PATRON OF
SHAKESPEARE and VIRGINIA

HENRY WRIOTHESLEY,
THE THIRD EARL OF SOUTHAMPTON

BRYAN DUNLEAVY

PATRON OF VIRGINIA AND SHAKESPEARE

HENRY WRIOTHESLEY,
THE THIRD EARL OF SOUTHAMPTON

BRYAN DUNLEAVY

Published by the Titchfield History Society 2023

ISBN 978-1-915166-07-4

PATRON OF SHAKESPEARE AND VIRGINIA

EARLY LIFE

The second earl of Southampton was still under house arrest when news reached him that his countess had given birth to a son on October 6th 1573. He was soon named Henry after his father. The birth occurred at Cowdray, the house of Viscount Montague at Midhurst in Sussex, where his mother had been living during her confinement. The new-born boy came into a family with one older sister, Mary.

The infant Henry may have stayed at Cowdray for some time. In the Autumn the earl was summoned to court, presumably to ensure that he had repented of his subversive folly, for in a letter dated 1 November 1573 it is evident that he and his wife were travelling to London together with his brother-in-law Anthony Browne and Jane his wife. It would appear too that the Southamptons returned to Cowdray and stayed there well into 1574, possibly only moving to Titchfield when the infant was a year old.

By the time he was four, in 1577, he must have noticed that all was not well with his parents. Both were self-willed and self-centred and both had personalities that were unwilling to give way. The earl was a proud and stiff-necked man who did not know how to compromise or even find common ground. His wife never saw herself as anything other than the aggrieved party.

Unfortunately for his own emotional well-being he was forced to take sides. His father banished his mother from his presence in 1579 and it appears that for the last year's of the second earl's life he would not allow his wife to see her son. She did try to use the boy as an intermediary by writing a letter to the earl to be delivered by her son and although the six year old boy took the letter to his father the earl refused to read it. After this the boy was entirely under his father's influence and unsurprisingly in the circumstances took his side. His mother wrote in a later letter "he was never kind to me" and we might trace the young Henry Wriothesley's own difficulties with women as a young man to these formative experiences.

During these years his father was preoccupied with his building work at Dogmersfield and it is probable that the boy lived there. At any rate there is no surviving reference to him during these years apart from a mention in his grandmother's will, 26th July 1574, making various bequests to "my Son's son, Harrye, Lord Wriothesley."

His separation from his mother came to an end in 1581 when his father died at the age of only 36. The boy was now the third earl of Southampton although he faced a long minority before he was able to come into his inheritance.

In 1581 the widowed countess immediately set about a legal struggle to secure her rights. Other interested parties stirred to secure the wardship. All of these manoeuvres may have passed over the head of the eight year old boy who was nonetheless the focus of all attention. Even so it took some time for the executors to arrive at proper assessment, which they recorded in a book called The Sale of the Wards. The yearly value of the widow's third, assigned to the countess, was £362 19s. 0¾d.; the lands assigned to the crown were valued at £370 16s. 8d.; and the land allowed to the minor earl was valued at £363 11s. 2¼d. The total income amounted to just over £1,000.

There are figures which assess the value of the Southampton estate, but, although they appear to be accurate, may be an undervaluation.

Accordingly, once the estate had been valued and divided into thirds, Lord Howard of Effingham was granted the wardship for the sum of £1,000. It was a good investment. Over the next 13 years he would be able to draw revenues of about £4,000 from one third of the estate. However, it does appear that Howard transferred the wardship to Lord Burghley, probably for a financial consideration, although there is no surviving documentation to attest to this. The arrangement was not unfavourable to the Earl of Southampton; he got probably the finest education available to a young man of his class at this time, and he made a lifelong friend of Robert Cecil, which probably saved him from following the earl of Essex to the executioner's block in 1599.

Burghley himself, a man of letters rather than a man of action, had noted the scandalous deficiency of education for wards when he became Master of the Wards in 1561 and set about doing something about it. As a general practice those who purchased wardships focused their attention on taking profit and minimising expenses, and one of the areas where they could safely cut back was the cost of tutors for their wards. Burghley therefore set up a school in his own house and hired some of the best tutors as instructors. He had, of course, a vested interest when his own children were young, but after they had grown, and when Southampton was in attendance, he continued to maintain the same high standards and to take a personal and active interest in his charges.

The Burghley household was firmly protestant. It was also a well-regulated and happy household, and this is worth mentioning. G P V Akrigg makes the interesting observation that Southampton was translated 'from a disorderly ill-managed household where an underling ruled, he passed to the machine-like good order of Cecil House.' It could not but have had an

4

effect on the bright and sensitive young boy. The Burghley marriage was a happy one. When he married Mildred Cooke she was already (unusually) an educated woman and they since both shared a love of learning and they got on well together, surely an eye-opener for Southampton who had only known quarrelling between his parents. One anonymous biographer, who had spent twenty four years in the Burghley household, left these admiring comments:

His kindness most expressed to children; to whom there was never a man more loving nor tender hearted. . . . And how aptly and merrily, he would talk with them; and such pretty questions, and witty allurements, as much delighted himself, the children, & the hearers.

While his parents were strong adherents to the Roman church the young earl was not hostile to Protestantism as an adult.

In 1585, at the age of 12, the young Southampton was sent to St John's College, Cambridge. This was a common enough age to begin University studies and they usually took their degrees at the age of 15. St John's, a newish college founded in 1511, was, by 1585, strongly Protestant and this may also have had an impact on Southampton's religious beliefs. One might detect Burghley's influence in the decision to send him there. At university he was taught rhetoric, logic, ethics, arithmetic, geometry, perspective, cosmography and also ancient and modern history, and it all had a theological dressing in the Protestant thinking of the day.

After taking his MA he entered Gray's Inn, near to Southampton House, to complete his education. Legal education of some sort was a final step in the preparation of the young Southampton for his coming into his inheritance. As a landowner who would undoubtedly be involved in legal transactions of one kind or another, he would obviously benefit from some knowledge, even though he would be able to employ specialist lawyers to do the necessary work. It has to be said that many of the young gentlemen who enrolled at the Inns of Court had little interest in hard study and much more interest in following the urges of their young manhood. In this respect they were not dissimilar to the Oxbridge Universities of three or four generations ago, where young men of wealth and status had a jolly good time and paid little attention to their studies. Serious study was left to those of less exalted backgrounds who had to put more effort into making their way in the world. We don't know in which camp Southampton found himself, but it is more likely than not that the attractions of the good time group were hard to resist.

It is tempting to imagine that the third earl's first exposure to the theatre occurred on the evening of 16 January 1588 at Gray's Inn where an unspecified comedy was enacted. It was a thoroughly respectable occasion with the Earls of Warwick, Leicester and Ormond in attendance together with Lord Burghley and Lord Grey of Wilton. It would have been here that he encountered the joys of the theatre. He was proposed by Lord Burghley to Gray's Inn on 29 February 1588. On the following day, the first day of March, he was admitted to the inn. Only the night before a play by Thomas Hughes, the Misfortunes of Arthur had been performed. Play performances at the Inns of Court were not uncommon.

It seems almost certain that these young bloods were regulars at the theatres when they were open and regularly trooped off as a group to the theatres across the river or in the suburbs. It is quite possible that he met William Shakespeare during these excursions.

The young earl emerges from the later years of his wardship as a highly intelligent and personable young man. Possibly his education in Burghley's school and at St Johns College Cambridge had developed a more rounded and more sociable personality than his rather moody father. Nevertheless there were still some traits of his father that were embedded in his personality, most particularly a certain stubbornness that set his face against more sensible behaviour. The first issue was that of marriage.

It was Burghley's intention, and indeed his right, to marry off his granddaughter Elizabeth de Vere to the young Southampton. Part of the arrangement that Burghley came to with Lord Howard of Effingham was that he would arrange the marriage of Southampton. This would in effect be the compensation for his trouble and expense in raising and educating the boy. They were close in age and of equivalent social standing, Elizabeth being the daughter of the Earl of Oxford. Despite the obvious self-interest for Lord Burghley it was judged a suitable match, not only in status, but also because it could bring additional wealth into the Wriothesley family. It is worth bearing in mind that the young earl inherited debts from his father and that he only had the income from one third of his estate to discharge them. This was not a matter for love but a matter for practical economics. The plan was sound and most Elizabethans would have agreed.

There was one problem - the young earl was not interested. When pressed, he took the line that he had no objection to this girl in particular, but he was not ready for marriage. Burghley persisted and enlisted the support of Southampton's mother and the ageing Viscount Montagu, his grandfather. Montagu discussed the matter with the young man and informed Burghley by letter that "this general answer that your Lordship was this last winter well pleased to yield unto him a further respite of one year to answer resolute in respect of his young years." This proposed compromise most likely came from Lord Montagu; the young man was not inclined to budge.

It has also been suggested that the Queen herself was brought in to advise the young man when she visited Titchfield at the end of August 1591. The queen's progress that Summer had taken her through Guildford and south to Cowdray for six days in August for some lavish entertainment. She then moved to Chichester, Portsmouth and then Titchfield 'for two standings for her Majesty.' From thence to be entertained by the bishop of Winchester at 'Bishop's Walton', presumably the palace at Bishop's Waltham, and then northwards to London.

In this matter he showed the same stubborn streak that had so characterised his father' behaviour. He was against marriage and would not be moved. He stood firm. Not even the queen could persuade him and in this respect Southampton was the loser; the queen never held him in much regard for the rest of her life.

At one level this independence was admirable, and with the benefit of the twentieth century study of psychology, we can understand the damage done to him by the venomous breakdown of his parents' marriage. It would be hard for the young man to see much personal advantage in marriage. Eventually Burghley found a suitable husband for his grand daughter in William Stanley, the new earl of Derby and a grand ceremony was held with the queen in attendance on 26 January 1595. One must assume that the outcome was satisfactory for Elizabeth de Vere.

It was much less so for the 3rd earl of Southampton. There was a high price to pay for this intransigence. In the first instance Burghley exacted a fine of £5,000 against Southampton in 1594, as he was legally entitled to do.

Southampton therefore came into his inheritance with an immediate bill of huge proportions, whatever the actual figure. This could be overcome in time. Of more lasting damage was his reputation with the Queen, who noted the young man's stubborn streak with disfavour. Nowadays this sort of principled stance would win him high plaudits; in Elizabethan times such action was regarded as foolhardy.

Even so, the 3rd earl in 1593 was on the verge of a rich inheritance. During the twelve years of his minority the estates had been competently managed and the debts of the 2nd earl had been squared.

COMING OF AGE

Henry Wriothesley was young, energetic and wanted to cut a figure in the world. Military service of some kind would have suited him well, particularly service under the bright star of the earl of Essex. There was indeed some prospect of this at the outset of 1591, when English foreign policy was leaning towards support of Henri IV of France against the catholic insurgency. There were some rumour that the earl of Essex would be sent over with a force and this may have prompted the impetuous Southampton to take matters into his own hands.

The Corporation of Southampton granted the earl the freedom of the town on 9 January 1591 and it was from Dieppe that he wrote to Essex in a letter dated 2 March. One guess is that he left Southampton port in January to be ready to be joined by the earl. This did not come to pass and he was ordered home in frustration. There must have been further frustration in the Summer when Essex was eventually sent over with a force of 3,000 men. The young earl was not one of them as his presence was required at Titchfield in September to entertain the queen.

There were other ways he could draw attention to himself. The Renaissance arrived later in England after its continental origins in Italy in the previous century, but by the second half of the century a young aristocrat was expected to demonstrate his intellectual credentials. men such as Sir Thomas Wyatt and the Earl of Surrey, became accomplished poets as well as statesmen, and young aristocrats of the next generation began to vie with one another to demonstrate their intellectual as well as physical accomplishments. The ideal for the age was held to be Sir Phillip Sidney, the soldier-poet. The Earl of Oxford, Edward de Vere, was a poet of some ability and he is now held by some to be the author of Shakespeare's plays. The claim of course is arguable, even preposterous, but the fact the de Vere wrote at all shows how important such accomplishments were for the Elizabethan aristocracy.

Another way of burnishing your intellectual credentials was to become a patron of the arts and young Southampton, with a decided interest in these matters, and coming into his majority, was a target for hopeful scribblers, including Shakespeare.

At some time, and certainly before 1592, William Shakespeare moved to London, where he became an actor. There is some evidence that he had ventured into writing plays, either in collaboration with others or independently and it was probably in this year that he was able to seek, and be granted, the patronage of the 3rd Earl of Southampton.

On the 18 April 1593 an entry was made at the Stationer's Register for a poem called Venus and Adonis. The printer was a man called Richard Field, whom Shakespeare knew from growing up in Stratford, and the dedication was to the 3rd. Earl of Southampton, couched in respectful language:

To the Right Honourable Henry Wriothesley, Earl of

Southampton, and Baron of Titchfield. Right Honourable, I know not how I shall offend in dedicating my unpolished lines to your Lordship, nor how the world will censure me for choosing so strong a prop to support so weak a burden, only, if your Honour seem but pleased, I account myself highly praised, and vow to make advantage of all idle hours, till I have honoured you with some graver labour. But, if the first heir of my invention prove deformed, I shall be sorry it had so noble a god-father, and never after ear so barren a land, for fear it would yield me still so bad a harvest. I leave it to your Honourable survey, and your Honour to your heart's content; which I wish may always answer your own wish, and the world's hopeful expectation. Your Honour's in all duty.

and signed by the then unknown William Shakespeare.

The earl was barely 20 years old and the provincial wordsmith, struggling to establish himself in the world of letters was a day or two shy of his 29th birthday. The younger man was at the top of the Elizabethan social order and William Shakespeare was practically a nobody. The poem was an immediate success. It marked out Shakespeare as a poet of rare talent and it brought kudos to the earl as a man who was able to identify a literary star.

The printed edition of the poem first became available in June 1593. It sold out very quickly and Field printed a second edition in 1594. He then sold the copyright to John Harrison who brought out a third edition in 1595. Demand did not abate and 16 known editions of the book were printed by 1640. Each printed volume was so much read and handled by so many readers that the few editions that survive today are in very poor condition. Shakespeare's story was sourced from Arthur Golding's translation of Ovid's Metamorphoses. The tale describes the pursuit of the beautiful mortal Adonis by Venus, the goddess of love. He resists her advances at first, but eventually succumbs to her charms and they spend 24 hours in each other's company, which ends when Adonis insists on hunting a boar despite warnings of the danger by Venus. He is killed by the boar and the love story thus has a tragic end. The atmosphere throughout the poem is sexually charged and it was this characteristic, unusual for the time, made it a "best seller" if that term can be applied to books in that period.

1594 was a seminal year for both the earl and William Shakespeare. The earl achieved his majority and a government rationalisation of control of the players' companies had the unintended consequence of making William Shakespeare and his player colleagues prosperous men. Theatres were not popular with the City of London authorities as they attracted crowds which facilitated the work of pickpockets and prostitutes, but the court had an interest in maintaining professional players for the occasional entertainment of the queen and the aristocracy. Lord Hunsdon, who was Lord Chamberlain at the time, developed a plan to allow two regulated companies and William Shakespeare became a sharer in one of these. This duopoly lasted beyond Shakespeare's life.

The earl formally reached the age of 21 on 6 October 1594, and although there are indications that he was already acting as if he was fully in control of his affairs throughout the year, the date was of great legal significance. A celebration was planned for this anniversary.

However, two nights earlier a sensational event was to overshadow the celebrations. Two close friends, the brothers Danvers, had been involved in the murder of a long time enemy. They fled to Titchfield and the earl was able to arrange for a ship to take them to France, and safety. A few years later they were allowed to return to England.1

It cannot be a coincidence that Shakespeare's play about feuding families, *Romeo and Juliet*, appeared the following year.

In addition to the Danvers brothers, Southampton's young friends included Roger Manners, who became the 5th Earl of Rutland. Manners had also become one of Burghley's wards after the death of his own father in 1588. Together, they formed a group of rich, boisterous young men who put their surplus energy into drinking, gaming, wenching and the pursuit of adventure. They were naturally frequent attenders of the theatres. The old queen, in the last decade of her long life, did not approve, and Southampton's association with these young bloods did nothing to advance his court career. The queen was now at an age when she preferred serious and sensible young men like Robert Cecil; the roisterers no longer delighted her. Efforts were made to guide these youthful aristocrats, including the Earl of Southampton, onto a more conventional path, but to no end. He was not ready.

When marriage did come, it was unplanned.

In September 1595 Henry began to pay attention to one of the Queen's maids of honour, Elizabeth Vernon. She was born in the same year as Southampton, 1573, and had been recommended for the Queen's service by the Earl of Essex, who was a first cousin. Her father had died in 1591, leaving a son and four daughters.

Even so, the earl was still not yet ready for marriage, and for that matter, could not afford it either, with heavy fines outstanding, so while there are indications that he continued to show an interest in Elizabeth Vernon, nothing was to come of it, for now.

Young aristocrats had limited options: they could quietly and diligently manage their estates, they could pursue a political career at court, or they could seek military glory. In some cases they might enjoy all three. The first course was the least risky and the second required mastery of the art of compromise. The third offered adventure, excitement and the prospect of fame and for a young man of the earl's age and temperament the draw was irresistible. He was disappointed in this ambition; he was destined to wait.

MILITARY EXPERIENCE

In the spring of 1596 Elizabeth authorised an expedition to attack Cadiz. Lord Admiral Howard, an experienced campaigner, and the Earl of Essex were given charge of the venture. This should have been an

---

1. The whole affair is described in the booklet, *How to Get Away with Murder.* *ISBN: 978-1-993421-35-8*

opportunity for Southampton and he would certainly have been selected by Essex, but the Queen still did not regard him favourably and it appears that he was not allowed to go. On 13 April the Queen sent specific instructions to Essex that he was only to take those men who had licence to travel - Sussex, Rich, Herbert and Burgh. Southampton was not on the list.

He was compelled to cool his heels in frustration, anxious for preferment but continued to be ignored until the Spring of 1597, when it was reported that he was finally granted leave to go to sea. There were complex preparations and delays but eventually, on 11 August, Elizabeth gave permission for Essex to attack the port of Ferrol on the north west coast of Spain. Sir Walter Raleigh was to lead part of the fleet but the Earl of Essex was in overall command. Southampton was among his young lieutenants.

Some ships were damaged in a storm in the Bay of Biscay and had to be sent home. As a consequence Essex decided that his fleet was not strong enough to attack Ferrol and as they sailed down the coast where they learned that the Spanish fleet had sailed to the Azores to escort ships home from America. Sensing an opportunity, they set direction for the Azores, where they succeeded in taking three treasure ships, one of them seized by Southampton, who was knighted by Essex for his enterprise. The remainder of the Spanish fleet escaped to harbour in Terceira, where they were protected. Essex decided that he was not strong enough to attack the port and set course for home with their booty. They were pursued by Spanish warships but they outran them. They reached England in late October.

If Southampton believed that his part in this broadly successful expedition would bring him into the royal sunlight, he was to be again disappointed. The political winds had changed at home and Essex's star was on the wane. Sir Robert Cecil had been appointed Chief Secretary to the Queen and was also made Chancellor of the Duchy of Lancaster, an office to which Essex aspired. Cecil was a supporter of Raleigh, at this time the great rival to Essex. The Queen was also displeased that Essex had knighted so many of his followers, including Southampton.

In January 1598 the earl might have looked forward to a bleak year. The Queen continued to be frosty towards him, his mother had been recently widowed for the second time and her second husband, Sir Thomas Heneage owed £528 18s. 1d. to the Treasury, and he was still under a debt burden due to the fine to Lord Burghley.

A trivial incident brought Southampton once again into disfavour with the queen. He was playing a card game called Primmer in the Queen's presence chamber. The queen had retired for the night, and Southampton,

Sir Walter Raleigh and a man named Parker continued playing. Ambrose Willoughby, an official, asked the men to stop the game as the Queen had gone to bed. Raleigh folded his cards, picked up his money and left, but Southampton took exception to the order and told Willoughby he would remember it. He did, and on another occasion, when they met in the garden, struck Willoughby and the two got into a scuffle before they were parted. The Queen, on hearing the story, took Willoughby's side and recorded a further black mark against Southampton.

Cecil must have decided that it were best for the young hothead to be out of the way. He was undertaking an embassy to France and procured a license for Southampton to accompany him. He was at this time actively courting Elizabeth Vernon and there was every expectation that they would marry.

Nevertheless, the earl was able to travel to Paris to meet up with his old friends, the Danvers brothers, who were spending fruitless time in exile after the murder of Henry Long in 1594. At this point the old friends planned a tour of Italy, but this adventure was interrupted by news from England that the two brothers would be pardoned as a result of an agreed settlement brokered with the Long family. This meant that the Danvers brothers had to return to England immediately.

Southampton was not far behind. His plan for a two year travel period was interrupted at the end of August by news that Elizabeth Vernon had had to leave court and take refuge in Essex House due to "an illness." The lady was pregnant.

There was only one way to put this right and at the beginning of September Southampton quietly returned to England, secretly married Elizabeth Vernon, and immediately returned to Paris. He had been noticed. The Queen was informed that he had 'privily' come to England and Cecil was instructed to deal with the matter. Cecil wrote a stiff letter to Southampton instructing him to see the Queen immediately. He returned in early November and he was sent to the Fleet prison for two weeks. Form was satisfied and the Queen turned to more important matters.

At 25, the earl was now married to a powerless woman and they had a daughter. He was heavily in debt. He was out of favour at Court. What were his prospects?

He had little choice but to continue to hitch his wagon to the splendid engine of the Earl of Essex.

THE EARL OF ESSEX

Robert Devereaux, Earl of Essex, was the stellar character of his time.

He was tall and had a commanding personality. He was highly intelligent and like most of those young people who had been a ward of Lord Burghley was well educated. But he was not merely well-versed in the academic knowledge of the day, he was also an accomplished writer and could turn his hand to verse or prose with a facility which was often better than some of the professional writers of his time. He loved action and adventure and in the military engagements of the day won fame and approbation. The Queen liked him and took him on as one of her favourites, in some ways replacing his ageing stepfather the Earl of Leicester. He was a most attractive man.

With these attributes it is not surprising that ambitious young men were drawn to this bright flame. He was a natural leader.

Yet for all his gifts Essex was flawed. Honours came easily to him and when things did not go his way he tended to behave petulantly. He became arrogant and was even at times offensive to the queen when she would not permit him to do as he wished. He was an aspirant to become the leading statesman of the realm, the only conceivable successor in his own mind to the venerable Lord Burghley. He possessed many of the gifts that would have served him well as a leader in the 16th century but he had no patience with the subtleties of politics and no understanding of any way but his way of doing things.

His victory at Cadiz in 1596 was justly applauded but while this was happening the hunchback Robert Cecil, the antithesis of the vigorous and handsome Essex, was stepping into his father's shoes. His preferment deeply rankled with the proud Essex who felt slighted and continued to be awkward. So when Ireland became an issue once again at the end of the century there were those on Council who were eager to push for Essex to lead the expedition. Ireland, as they well knew, had been a political graveyard for many in the past and an actual graveyard for some.

One night in 1598 the poet Edmund Spenser had to flee for his life from his home at Kilcoman Castle due to a general uprising by the Irish against the English. Spenser had first gone to Ireland in 1580 and while there wrote his most famous work of poetry, *The Faerie Queene*. He had prospered in Ireland but his hurried departure left him completely destitute - homeless, landless and without any source of income. He died on 13 January 1599. He was only 46 and Ben Jonson later wrote that he died "for want of bread."

The Irish problem began some years earlier when Turlough O'Neill handed over the chieftainship of Ulster to his cousin Hugh, Earl of Tyrone. The new O'Neill had been educated in England and was a very sophisticated man. The English would have considered him to be a safe pair of hands but he confounded all when he decided to embrace the Irish cause once he became "The O'Neill." Tyrone formed an alliance with the neighbouring O'Donnell clan and arranged for money to be sent from Spain, who were only too happy to destabilise Elizabeth's government. He bought good weapons and trained his Irish soldiers in contemporary warfare. Before long he had built up a formidable fighting machine and at the Battle of Yellow Ford 15 August 1598, he routed the English army. This success encouraged other clans in Ireland and poor Spenser, living near Cork, became one of the casualties.

The English garrison in Ireland had been reduced to little more than the Pale around Dublin, and Elizabeth was faced with larger problems than the fate of Edmund Spenser. If Ireland was lost it would quickly become a base for King Phillip of Spain and that outcome would be serious. A call went out to the shires to raise a large force, and after some political wrangling, Essex was chosen to lead the invading army. He was not altogether enthusiastic. He had lost some of his lustre after the last Spanish expedition and he knew as well as anyone the perils of warfare in Ireland. Nevertheless he agreed.

Essex received his commission as viceroy and commander in chief in Ireland on 12 March and the expedition started from London on 27 March 1599. Southampton must have been overjoyed at the opportunity to finally achieve his youthful ambition of military service. He was first among Essex's array of young officers, which included the Earl of Rutland, Charles and Henry Danvers and Lord Grey. With the exception of Lord Grey the group were very much united by kinship and friendship and were very much the core of the Essex circle. They arrived, not without a difficult sea crossing, on 4 April. The intention of the expedition was to subdue the Earl of Tyrone's rebellion in Ulster. On 15 April Essex appointed Southampton as "Lord General of the Horse in Ireland." Sir Henry Danvers, Southampton's long-time friend was made "Lieutenant of the Horse: and the Earl of Rutland was appointed "Lieutenant General of the Infantry."

Essex's mission was to destroy the Tyrone uprising in the north but when he reached Dublin that Spring he was advised that there would not be enough forage for horses or food for the army in the north immediately after winter and he was counselled against such an expedition. He decided, probably correctly, to use his army to bring Leinster and Munster under control, and on 9 May he moved west to Athy, where the garrison was surrendered without contest. Southampton travelled north west to Maryborough with about 160 horse. There he was challenged by about 200 mounted Irishmen. He did lead a successful charge against the Irish and after the skirmish the Irish retreated.

Then a quarrel broke out between Southampton and Lord Grey of Wilton. At Maryborough, Grey decided to freelance and led a charge against the retreating Irish despite orders not to engage. Southampton rightly reproved him and disciplined him by placing him under arrest overnight. Grey was incensed at what he saw as a humiliation and was ever after an enemy of Southampton. Grey was not the forgiving type nor would he meekly conform to Southampton's authority. At a battle at Fermoy on the return journey Grey led a charge of the vanguard cavalry against some rebels who were seemingly in retreat. Unfortunately this was a deliberate tactic by the Irish; once the vanguard had been drawn off, the main Irish force attacked the baggage train and it took fierce fighting, during which Sir Henry Danvers was injured in the face, for Essex to bring his forces safely through. Soon after, Grey returned to England and was able to give his version of events to the Queen where he found a willing ear.

The Queen sent a blistering letter to Essex making her feelings plain in a letter of July 19th.

Essex had little choice but to comply with the command and remove Southampton from his position. It was a small victory for Grey, but Essex did not abandon his friend; he simply abolished the position of General of the Horse and allowed Southampton to continue with his duties. As a captain, Southampton continued to serve his leader and friend.

The campaign to subdue the two southern Irish provinces largely achieved its objective. The force moved west to Limerick and returned via Waterford and Wicklow to Dublin, arriving there on 2 July. Later that month there was a shorter expedition into Offaly.

While military tacticians might endorse Essex's sensible approach, the council in London, particularly those members hostile to Essex placed their own interpretation on events. The message that they chose to receive was that he was frivolously wasting his time on targets which in any case could have been dealt with by the resident garrison in the Pale of Dublin. The queen wrote angry letters to him in July condemning his inaction and withdrawing his licence to return, which had been included in the original indenture. Essex now felt that he had been exiled indefinitely, and was possibly in a similar position to Richard, Duke of York in 1450.

He was now in a difficult situation. With a small army of perhaps 3,000 - 4,000 at his disposal, a shortage of supplies and the prospect of facing a larger force in Ulster, his army council, all experienced officers, agreed that they had little hope of success. Nevertheless Essex set out with his force on 2 September. A few days later he met for a parley with Hugh O'Neill, Earl of Tyrone, and on 8 September they agreed to a truce to last for the winter. Essex then returned to Dublin with his army.

Essex had defied the queen but he hoped that he could justify his action, so he left Dublin and arrived in London on 28 September. He burst into Elizabeth's bedchamber before she had had a chance to dress to give her the news. This now elderly woman, without make-up, was much affronted by the intrusion and Essex was ordered to keep to his chamber while the council met. The following morning he was questioned by the council for three hours. It appears that he made a good case for himself, since the majority of the council favoured lenient treatment and release. The queen however was not to be appeased and he was committed to the custody of Sir Thomas Egerton.

Tyrone of course broke the truce and Essex's efforts came to nothing; nor did this do anything to improve the queen's temper and he remained a prisoner for almost a year and was also deprived of various offices. Eventually, on 26 August 1600, he gained his freedom. He was now a bitter man and his mind turned to plot and rebellion. Essex House became a gathering place for discontents whether they be puritan or papists. He called his close friends, Henry Wriothesley, Sir Charles Danvers, Sir Ferdinand Gorges and Sir John Davies to organise a plan. The plan was to seize the council and pressure the queen into following their agenda. There was now confusion and a failure of nerve. The original plot was discarded in favour of improvisation. Essex would come to London with 200 armed men and, with the expectation of strong popular support in London, would be able to press his case. In the event the citizens of London were surprised, amazed and uncomprehending. There was no popular support. This was not 1399, when a popular duke was seeking to claim his rightful inheritance from a tyrannical king. While Elizabeth might be old and tired, she was not unpopular enough for people to welcome deposition. The government put up barricades and Essex was forced to retreat by water and find his way back to his house outside the city walls. Government troops then surrounded the house and he was forced to surrender. He was arrested with others, including Southampton..

They were tried on 19 February 1601. Essex, Danvers, Blount, Cuff and Merck were sentenced to death but Southampton was surprisingly spared.

There appears to have been some residual sympathy for Southampton as perhaps illustrated in Robert Cecil's letter to George Carew in March: "It remaineth now that I let you known what is like to become of the poor young Earl of Southampton, who, merely for the love of the Earl has been drawn into this action." It is likely that Cecil's intervention saved Southampton. He had been condemned to death along with the others but now he was merely left to languish in prison, a state of affairs that lasted until the queen's death.

A FRESH START

He was in luck.

Time eventually caught up with the ageing queen. She died at about 2 a.m. on 24 March 1603, coincidentally, the very last day of the old calendar year. Lady Day, 25 March, the traditional beginning of a new year, was seen to carry good omens for a better future. The old queen's reign, for all of the glorification of the 'Elizabethan Age', had become tired and stale in her final decade: hence the impatience of the Earl of Essex and his young followers, one of whom was languishing in the Tower and who had great hopes for the accession of the king of Scotland.

He was not out of tune with the times. Sir Robert Cecil, the Howard family and many of the centrist English nobles supported the Stuart accession. In addition, James, waiting impatiently in Scotland, had been very much in sympathy with Essex and his followers. So one of James' first acts before leaving Scotland for Westminster, was to sign an order for the release of Southampton. Southampton was at last at liberty.

On 16 May the king granted Southampton a full pardon. This meant that he could resume the title of earl and that his lands would be restored to him. Even better, he was rewarded with the Captaincy of the Isle of Wight, worth 6,000 crowns a year. He was formally re-created Earl of Southampton and Baron Titchfield at a ceremony at Hampton Court on 21 July.

Southampton was awarded the farm of sweet wines. This was a slight refinement on the old medieval practice of assigning tax gathering to a noble on behalf of the king. In previous practice money was gathered and an acceptable amount was paid to the treasury while the collector retained what he could. In this new model Southampton was granted the rights to levy import duties on sweet wine, and for this he paid an annual rent to the crown of £6,000. He could then make from the franchise what he could. The farm had been worth £2,500 a year to the earl of Essex and when Southampton later surrendered it to the Crown in 1611 he was given a pension of £2,000 a year in compensation, so one must assume that it was worth at least that amount.

The earl had bounced back. While Elizabeth was alive he was living in the Tower with a much reduced income as a consequence of his youthful extravagance, but by August of 1603 he was in a position to double his income! There was no longer any need to live a constrained and frugal life.

A year after Southampton's liberation the Countess was brought to bed to give birth to their second child. It was another daughter. Her precise date of birth is unknown but she was baptised in April 1604 in the Chapel at Whitehall. Queen Anne stood as a godparent and the baby was named Anne, in honour of her godmother. In the following year, on 1 March 1605 an heir to the earldom was born and he was baptised on 27 March. He was named James in honour of the king. On 10 March 1607, a second son joined the family. He was named Thomas after the founding earl.

There were more land sales in this period. Great Compton was sold for

£2,000 and Romsey Extra for £450. He purchased Fairthorne Manor at Botley but then had to sell it in 1611. Four other Hampshire manors were sold at the same time. These sales were probably necessary to raise money for his daughters' marriage portions. He had to put up £4,000 to marry his eldest daughter Penelope to Lord Spencer. The marriage portion for his second daughter is unknown.

Royal favour translated into the largest part of Southampton's income between 1603 and 1621. In addition to the lucrative farm for sweet wines he held the Keepership of the New Forest, Vice Admiralty of Hampshire, Governorship of the Isle of Wight and James also granted him pensions and other sums for unknown reasons. Lawrence Stone has estimated that his Crown income during these years was £1,500 a year at a minimum and may have been as high as £4,000. The income from his estates, as we have discussed, jogged along at about £2,000 a year. On balance, it can be said that he could afford to live very well on £6,000 a year. He could also afford to invest periodic sums of £500 and £1,000 in the Virginia company explorations. It is almost impossible to determine whether or not he got any return on that investment.

A COLONIAL PIONEER

One striking characteristic of the third earl was his intellectual interest in new ventures. The humdrum management of his estates did not excite him and he was content to leave matters to his stewards to carry on much as before. What did get his juices flowing was any prospect of a new and exciting venture. The exploration and settlement of the North American coast captured his imagination and he became a leading participant in the Virginia Company.

This was a period when many Englishmen were attracted by the prospect of colonising the 'new world.' Early settlements had not been successful but this did not deter new investors, including the Earl of Southampton.

In 1609 a charter was given to the Virginia Company with full power to govern the colony. No fewer than 650 individuals and 56 city companies were anxious to subscribe. At the head of the list was Lord de la Warr, putting up £500, the Earl of Pembroke, who committed £400 and the Earl of Southampton who contributed £350. Lord de la Warr was to be the Governor, but he sent a deputy, Sir Thomas Gates in his place. Nine ships sailed from Plymouth carrying 600 colonists.

The voyage was not without incident. The fleet encountered a hurricane. The leading vessel, the Sea Venture, was washed up on the shore of Bermuda, where, without loss of life, the stranded mariners were able to survive the winter with a plentiful supply of food. The remainder of the fleet reached the mainland. The story, when it reached England, was to inspire The Tempest, one of Shakespeare's last plays.

Once discovered, this island, later known as Bermuda, became a target for colonists and the Somers Island or Bermuda Company was established in 1615. Southampton was a founding investor.

The new Virginia settlement ran into the now familiar problem of lack of effective leadership. Various attempts were made to overcome this problem but successive expeditions over the decade brought poor returns on the investment. Eventually, company leaders resolved on a change of policy. All settlers would be granted 50 acres. This appeared to work and the new crop of tobacco was able to feed a growing habit in Europe. Finally a cash crop! The colony did not exactly thrive during this period but it did at last provide some return for the investors. The '50 acre' policy salvaged the enterprise.

Even so, it a smaller and less well-funded expedition of three ships sailing from Southampton and Plymouth in September 1620 that is remembered in history. The so-called Pilgrim Fathers landed at Cape Cod in what was later to be called the state of Massachusetts. This voyage was successful because these colonists were highly disciplined and led by men who forced the settlers to conform and protect themselves against winter. The earlier settlers of Virginia were still struggling to understand how they could effectively organise their new society.

The company was in serious difficulty in the 1620s. There had been huge investment and the company was £5,000 in debt. Various factions within the company fell to arguing and recrimination and the king decided to intervene and the upshot was that the charter was removed in April 1624. After 18 years and the expenditure of a great deal of money and considerable loss of life the failed venture was over.

There was some sort of legacy from this. Southampton held title to land in Virginia and Colonel William Byrd was able to buy these lands from the estate of the 4th earl, who did not share his father's interest in the New World. Southampton is now remembered by a county in Virginia and a town on the island of Bermuda.

AN EARLY INDUSTRIALIST

The third earl's restless curiosity for the new and modern did not lie solely with exotic lands across the ocean. Closer to home he established an ironworks.

Roger Manners, Earl of Rutland and bosom friend of the 3rd Earl of Southampton took an interest in his family's acquisition of Rievaulx Abbey in North Yorkshire, principally because the land included medieval ironworks. Rutland developed these ironworks with some success and his friend, ever curious about new ventures decided to emulate this venture on the south coast.

He may have started on this project soon after his release from the Tower in 1603 because by 1605 there were already complaints about the demand for wood creating a fuel shortage. He established a furnace at Sowley on the Beaulieu estate and another at Funtley on the Meon. The Sowley furnace was able to access ironstone from Hengistbury Head and Hordle Cliffs. Both furnace locations had access to a large supply of wood and both could use the rivers for shipping. The Sowley furnace produced pig iron, which was then shipped to Funtley to be refined into wrought iron.

He was initially ambitious for the project and must have planned for expansion. When he leased the Botley Flour Mill in 1608 he inserted a clause that allowed him to cancel the lease should he decide to build an ironworks there instead. The option was never taken up and it must have become apparent to the earl that the potential profits were limited in what had become a crowded market. In 1622 he abandoned direct management and granted a seven year lease of the furnaces at Sowley and Funtley for £103 a year. These lease arrangements continued in one form or another into the 18th century.

In the year before his death the earl was attracted to another venture, that of manufacturing tin plate. From a letter dated 1623 we learn that John Tite had gone into partnership with the earl to manufacture tin plate. In the letter he wrote: "The mill which batters the iron is the Earl's of Southampton, he hath been at a £1,000 charge to build it and to fit it for this work." There was agreement that a sum of £500 would launch the project and the earl contributed £200 for half the profit; the other half being shared by Tite and his active partner Thomas Jupp. It can be inferred that the mill was built at Wickham from a document of 1647.

How much these industrial ventures contributed to the earl's income is largely a matter of guesswork. The iron mills by 1624 only brought in £100 a year and the proceeds from the tin plate mill at Wickham are unknown. Lawrence Stone conjectures that the total income from these ventures could be no more than £400 for £500 a year.

MATTERS OF STATE

Although James had released him from his imprisonment in the Tower in 1603 and made him a Privy Councillor, and he appeared to be in favour, he was never quite at the centre of government. He was perhaps too independent-minded to suit James' style of kingship but there seems little doubt, once we examine Southampton's mature years, that he turned himself into a very skilful politician and contrived to become an effective voice even though the tide of English politics was heading towards doom. Rowse characterises him as a "leader of the Opposition" and there is some validity in this observation, but we must be careful in going too far with this comparison. English politics had yet to crystallise into government and opposition parties. Loyalties could be very fluid and personal.

Robert Cecil, 1st Earl of Salisbury, was the leading politician who stayed at the forefront of two regimes until the last year of his life. After he died in 1612, the kingdom slid towards ruin.

Cecil was replaced as Lord Treasurer by Charles Howard, the Earl of Nottingham, and he held that position until he resigned in 1619.

Southampton could have been a sensible replacement but George Villiers had became the king's favourite. Once he captured the king's attention in 1614 he was promoted rapidly though the nobility, becoming, baron, viscount, earl and marquess in rapid succession. By the time he was appointed Lord Treasurer in 1619 he was Marquess of Buckingham.

Buckingham favoured his relatives in various corrupt activities and was himself not slow in lining his own nest. He also had a taste for foreign adventure, something that James was careful to avoid, nevertheless, in James' declining years he was able to promote the expedition to Holland in 1624, that was fatal for the earl of Southampton.

An Untimely Death

Since he came to the throne in 1603, James had managed to steer clear of war, but in the last year of his life he was a sick man and had effectively abdicated his role to his son and his favourite "Steenie", the Duke of Buckingham. Foreign policy was therefore in the hands of this unwise duo. An attempt to secure an alliance with Spain through marriage in 1623 was something of a debacle and foreign policy swivelled to a French alliance soon after. In the course of negotiating the marriage of Charles and Henrietta Maria, Buckingham agreed to support the Dutch in their struggle for independence against the Spanish. A treaty with the Dutch was concluded in June 1624 and 6,000 volunteers were agreed to fight for the States General in Holland.

This had been the first opportunity for the Earl of Southampton to undertake military service since 1599 when he was part of Essex's Irish expedition, and where he had demonstrated some ability as a military commander. He must have looked forward to the new adventure. He raised his levy and departed for Holland on 7 August 1624. He took with him his eldest son James, who was also keen for the experience and they were able to meet Elizabeth, the exiled Queen of Bohemia. Thereafter not much is known. There were no military engagements, and the soldiers spent boring and idle hours in military camps. The curse of confined army life, dysentery, spread throughout the encampments and many soldiers lost their lives without ever seeing armed struggle. James Wriothesley was one of that number and he gave up his life on 5 November at Rosendaal. His father contracted the same illness but, apparently having overcome the fever, left Rosendaal with the intention of returning to England with his son's body. However at Bergen-op-Zoom on 10 November he collapsed and died. Both bodies were carried by sea to Southampton.

It was an unlucky end.

The bodies of the two men were interred at Saint Peter's Church,

Titchfield on 28 December 1624 in the vault commissioned by the 2nd earl. No monumental figures were added.

The Church Register has the entry:

> December 1624. The Right Honourable Henry Earle of Southampton, Knight of the most noble Order of the Garter, and one of his Majesties most Honourable Privy Council, was buried the 28th day of this month.